SKYSCRAPERS

A TRUE BOOK

by

Elaine Landau

Children's Press®
A Division of Scholastic Inc.

New York Toronto London Auckland Sydney
Mexico City New Delhi Hong Kong
Danbury, Connecticut

A skyscraper under construction

Author's Dedication:

For Areilla Garmizo

Library of Congress Cataloging-in-Publication Data

Landau, Elaine.
    Skyscrapers / by Elaine Landau.
        p. cm. — (A True Book)
    Includes bibliographical references and index.
    ISBN 0-516-22184-1 (lib. bdg.)   0-516-27324-8 (pbk.)
    1. Skyrscrapers—Juvenile literature. 2. Skyscrapers—Design and con-
struction—Juvenile literature. [1. Skyscrapers.] I. Title. II. Series.
NA6230 .L36 2001   720'.483—dc21
                                                          00-031392

    3 4 5 6 7 8 9 10 R 10 09 08 07 06 05 04 03

Contents

Towering Giants   5

From the Ground Up   10

Out of the Ashes   20

Reaching New Heights   28

The Race Is On!   36

To Find Out More   44

Important Words   46

Index   47

Meet the Author   48

King Kong clings to
a skyscraper.

Towering Giants

King Kong clung to one. Superman leaped over them. Kids love to ride in elevators up to the top of them. Have you ever been in an extremely tall building? One that towers far above the rest? If so, it was probably a skyscraper.

Skyscrapers seem to touch the sky. Most are at least thirty-five floors high, and some have more than one hundred floors. Many skyscrapers are more than just tall, however. Often these towering buildings house hotels, restaurants, and stores along with hundreds of offices. A skyscraper is like a small world in itself.

These tall buildings have changed our cities. Skyscrapers allow companies to employ more people than ever before.

These skyscrapers appear to brush up against the clouds.

People returning to work at a skyscraper

Imagine thousands of people going to work at the same address! With skyscrapers, many people can live and work in a small area.

The first skyscrapers were built in the United States. Their popularity has spread over the years. Now you can find these towering giants in cities around the world.

A skyscraper in Bogota, Colombia

From the Ground Up

A skyscraper has two main parts. One is the substructure or foundation. You do not see that part—it lies beneath the ground. The foundation is made of steel or sometimes concrete columns called piles and it stands on a layer of solid rock or soil. The

The future home
of a skyscraper

foundation helps bear the
building's weight.

The other part of a sky-
scraper is the superstructure.

Workers on a steel frame of a skyscraper

That is the aboveground portion of the building. In a one- or two-story structure, the walls hold up the building.

A skyscraper needs a steel- or steel-and-concrete-frame to hold it up. This frame is sometimes called a skeleton frame.

In some ways, a skyscraper's frame acts like a human skeleton. Your skeleton is made up of bones. It provides a frame for your body. A skeleton frame does the same for a skyscraper. The building's walls are attached to the outside of the frame. You cannot see the frame when the building is

This skyscraper's walls have begun to hide its frame.

completed. Like your skeleton, the frame is in there—doing its job.

Lots of planning goes into building a skyscraper. First, a site has to be chosen. Then architects and engineers work together to design the building. The architect decides on the skyscraper's shape and the

Architects and engineers talk about the plans for a new skyscraper.

materials to be used to build it. The engineer determines how to make the skyscraper strong enough to withstand natural forces, such as storms and earthquakes.

Strong winds can be a problem too. The force of the wind on a building is known as the wind load. A skyscraper must not sway too much in the wind. Too much swaying could affect the elevators' operation. It could also crack

The cracks in this skyscraper were caused by an earthquake.

the glass on the outside of the building.

Sometimes a model of the building is made and placed

in a wind tunnel. Winds from all directions are blown on the model at various speeds. This helps the engineers to see how the building will hold up under different wind conditions.

Engineers and architects also use computer models to learn about the building. These can help them make the best decisions in determining the shape of the building or how the windows should be placed. A good deal of time and effort

An architect examines a computer model of a building.

goes into designing and building skyscrapers, but the rewards are sky-high!

Out of the Ashes

Skyscrapers got their start in Chicago, Illinois, after a terrible fire. In October 1871, an uncontrollable blaze swept through the city. About 17,000 homes and other buildings were destroyed, leaving more than 90,000 people homeless.

That tragic fire set the stage for the birth of the skyscraper. With the city in ruins, the build-ings needed to be replaced,

A city block destroyed in the fire.

but land prices were high. Taller buildings gave people more room for homes and offices while using less land.

Steel skeleton frames had also just been invented. That meant bigger buildings could be safer too. Elevators were becoming popular then as

Workers begin to rebuild Chicago.

well. Employees could not be expected to walk up that many flights of stairs to get to work—they would be worn out before they even reached their desks.

The world's first skyscraper was only ten stories tall. Known as the Home Insurance Company Building, it was erected in Chicago in 1885. A talented engineer and architect named William Le Baron Jenney designed the building.

Home Insurance
Company Building

William Le Baron Jenney

Jenney is now considered a pioneer of early skyscraper design. He is sometimes called "the father of the skyscraper."

Within the next ten to fifteen years, a number of other skyscrapers were built. Many of these were in Chicago. The tallest of the early skyscrapers was the Masonic Temple built in Chicago in 1892. The structure had twenty-two stories. For a short period, it was the world's tallest building. No one imagined how small it would seem in the years to come.

Reaching New Heights

As time passed, skyscrapers continued to crop up in cities. Some of these buildings were highly unusual. They attracted a lot of attention and became extremely well known. One of these was the Flatiron Building. Built in New York City in 1902, the building looks like a triangle-

shaped tower. Its strange
shape surprised people since
no one had seen a building
that looks like the Flatiron.

29

Photographers from around the world have taken pictures of it. Young women walking past it were warned to be careful. Sometimes the downdrafts, or downward air currents, caused by the tall building would lift their skirts a bit.

More skyscrapers had gone up in New York City in the late 1800s. The city was becoming an important center for business and trade. Many New York businessmen felt these tall towers would make their city seem

more important. They wanted
New York to have more than
Chicago had. Besides, the
Mohawk Indians lived in New
York State. Many of them were
famous for their ability to keep

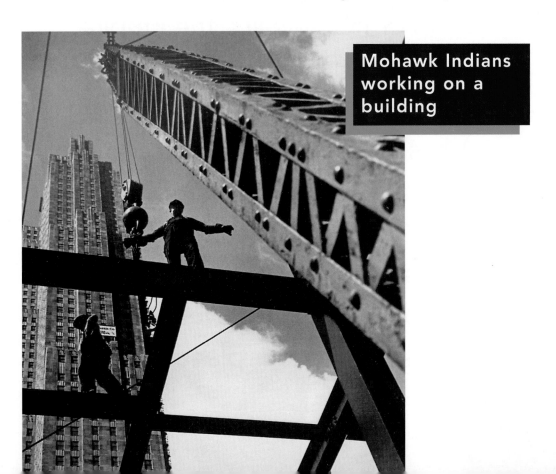

Mohawk Indians
working on a
building

their balance at great heights. They made outstanding sky-scraper builders. They helped bring New York City to even greater heights.

For many years, the Empire State Building in New York City was the world's tallest building. It has 102 stories, and stands 1,250 feet (381 meters) tall. Built in 1931, the Empire State Building was designed to withstand just about anything—even a plane. In 1945, a bomber plane actually

The Empire State Building (left); The bomber plane that crashed into the Empire State Building left this hole (below).

did crash into the seventy-ninth floor, and only two floors were damaged in the accident.

A view of New York City from the Empire State Building

From the Empire State Building's Observation Deck, at the building's top, you can see for 80 miles (129 kilometers).

Some claim that, on a clear day, you can see five states. There are taller skyscrapers today. Yet the Empire State Building is still considered a very huge building. Fifteen thousand people work there every day. There are 7 miles (11 km) of elevator shafts in the building. It also has 70 miles (113 km) of water pipes. The Empire State Building remains a sight most visitors to New York City do not want to miss.

The Race Is On!

As the decades passed, skyscraper technology (or know-how) advanced. Armed with better steel and improved construction methods, builders wanted to create even bigger skyscrapers.

In 1972, New York City's World Trade Center replaced

Skyscrapers
kept growing
over the years.

The World Trade Center before September 11, 2001

the Empire State Building as the world's tallest building. The World Trade Center stood on a 16-acre (6.5-hectare) site with twin towers that rose 1,350 feet

(411.5 m). On September 11, 2001, terrorists flew two airplanes into the twin towers. Shortly after the planes crashed, the World Trade Center buildings collapsed.

Then, in 1974, the Sears Tower in Chicago became the world's tallest building at 1,454 feet (443 m). It is made up of nine towers. They combine to form a single building. The floor area of the Sears Tower is equal to about

The Sears Tower in Chicago (below); From the top of the Sears Tower, you can see for miles and miles (right).

65 football fields. The Sears Tower is so huge that it has its own zip code.

About 1 1/2 million people visit the Sears Tower each year. They take high-speed elevators to the Skydeck—103 floors in 70 seconds—where they can enjoy the fabulous views. On a clear day, you can see for 50 miles (80 km) and get a glimpse of four states—Indiana, Illinois, Michigan, and Wisconsin.

Right now, the Petronas Towers skyscraper in Kuala Lumpur, Malaysia, is in the lead, being 1,483 feet (452 m) tall. This building won the race by putting an antenna on top that reaches higher than Sears Tower. The Petronas Towers may not hold the record for the world's tallest building for long, though. With several new buildings already underway to top the Petronas Towers, we are sure to have many more skyscrapers in our future.

The Petronas Towers in Kuala Lumpur, Malaysia

To Find Out More

Here are some additional resources to help you learn more about skyscrapers:

 **Books**

Dunn, Andrew. **Skyscrapers**. Thomson Learning, 1993.

Holland, Gini. **The Empire State Building.** Raintree Steck-Vaughn, 1998.

Hunter, Ryan Ann. **Into the Sky.** Holiday House, 1998.

Oxlade, Chris. **Skyscrapers and Towers.** Raintree Steck-Vaughn, 1997.

Richardson, Joy. **Skyscrapers.** Franklin Watts, 1994.

Organizations and Online Sites

Empire State Building
http://www.esbnyc.com/
Read all about the classic skyscraper that was once the world's tallest building.

Great Buildings
http://www.greatbuildings.com
Visitors to this online site can explore many of the world's greatest buildings, including the Sears Tower.

Sears Tower
http://www.sears-tower.com
Discover the history behind one of Chicago's most important landmarks.

The Skyscraper Museum
http://www.skyscraper.org
Learn more about high-rise buildings—their past, present, and future.

Important Words

downdraft downward current of air

foundation the part of a tall building that is beneath the ground helping to support the building's weight

piles the steel or concrete columns that make up a building's foundation

skeleton framework the steel or steel and concrete framework that supports tall buildings

skyscraper the name given to very tall buildings

substructure the part of a very tall building that is below ground

superstructure the part of a very tall building that is above ground

wind load the force of the wind on a building

Index

(**Boldface** page numbers
   indicate illustrations.)

Bogota, Colombia, **9**
Chicago, Illinois, 20, 25,
   27, 39
computer models, 18, **19**
downdraft, 30, 46
earthquake, 16, **17**
elevators, 16, 23
Empire State Building,
   32, 33, **33**, 34, **34**, 35,
   38
Flatiron Building, 28–29,
   29, 30
foundation, 10–11, 46
Home Insurance
   Company Building, 24,
   25
Jenney, William Le
   Baron, 25, 26, **26**
King Kong, **4,** 5
Kuala Lumpur, Malaysia,
   42

Masonic Temple, 27
Mohawk Indians, 31, **31,**
   32
New York City, 28–39
Petronas Towers, 42, **43**
piles, 10, 46
Sears Tower, 39, **40,** 41
skeleton framework, 13,
   46
skyscraper
   birth of, 20–21
   definition of, 46
   effect on cities, 6, 8
   parts of, 10
   planning to build,
      14–19
   withstanding natural
      forces, 16
substructure, 10, 46
superstructure, 11–12,
   46
wind load, 16, 46
World Trade Center, 36,
   38, **38,** 39

Meet the Author

Award-winning author Elaine Landau worked as a newspaper reporter, an editor, and a youth-services librarian before becoming a full-time writer. She has written more than one hundred and fifty nonfiction books for young people, including True Books on dinosaurs, animals, countries, and food.

Ms. Landau, who has a bachelor's degree in English and journalism from New York University and a master's degree in library and information science from Pratt Institute, lives in Florida with her husband and son.

Photographs ©: Corbis-Bettmann: 9 (The Purcell Team), 22, 23, 25, 31, 33 right; Dembinsky Photo Assoc.: 40 inset (Stephen Graham); Liaison Agency, Inc.: 2 (Craig J. Brown), 12 (Stephenie Hollyman), 40 (Jonathan Kirn), 19 (Wernher Krutein), 17 (Theodora Litsios), 33 left, 38 (Masumi Nakada), 15 (Jonathan E. Pite); Photofest: 4; Stock Montage, Inc.: 21; Stone: 7 (Ken Biggs), cover (Fred George), 14 (John Lamb), 37 (Peter Pearson), 29 (Joseph Pobereskin), 1 (Mark Segal); The Image Works: 43 (Bill Bachman), 34 (Bob Daemmrich), 8 (Frank Pedrick), 11 (M. Siluk), 26.